LIFE AT THE POLES

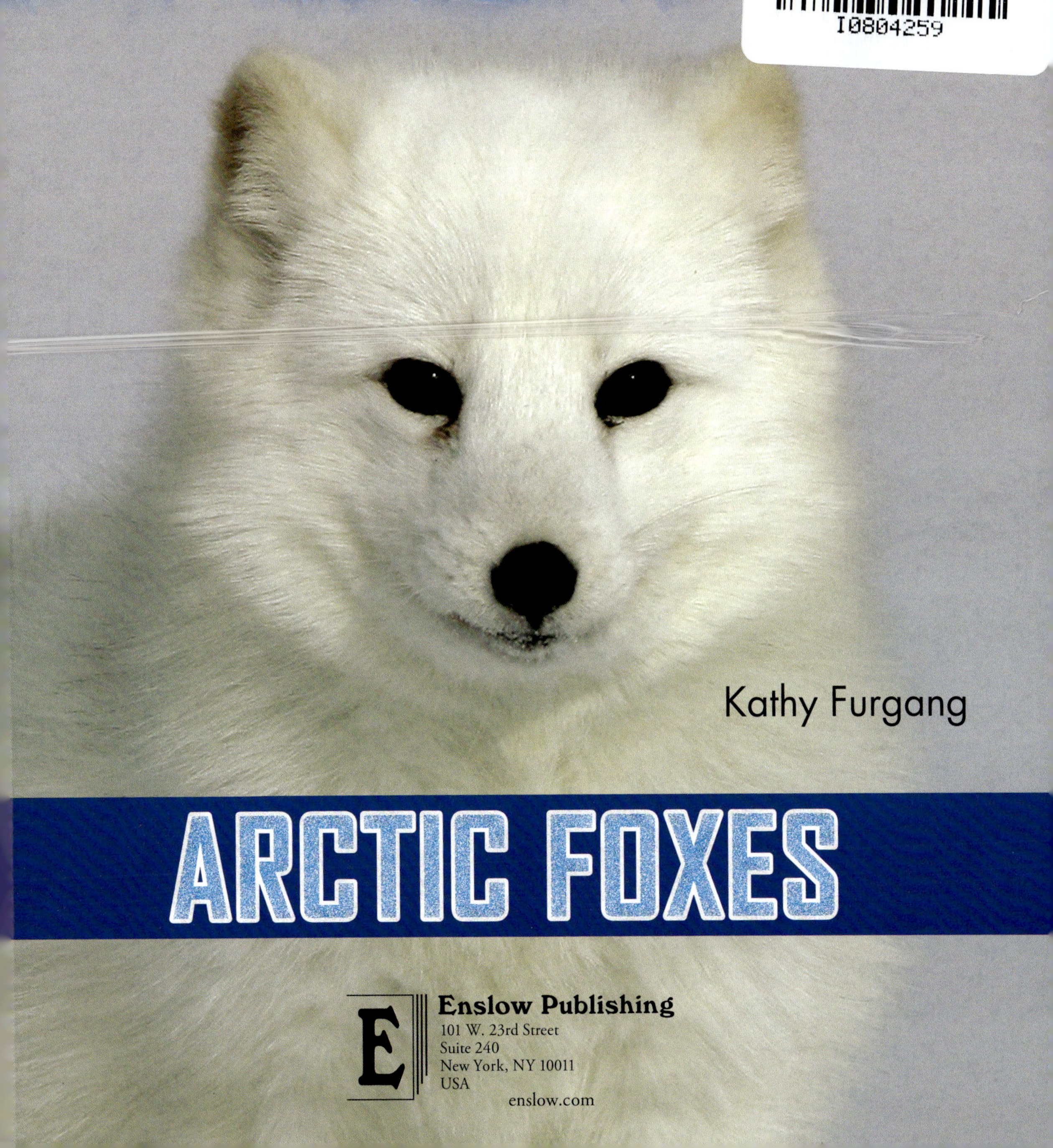

Kathy Furgang

ARCTIC FOXES

Enslow Publishing
101 W. 23rd Street
Suite 240
New York, NY 10011
USA
enslow.com

Words to Know

adaptation A change made by living things to help them survive better in an environment.

Arctic The part of the world that is farthest north, which includes the North Pole.

blizzard A strong winter storm that includes very high winds.

camouflage The color or pattern of a plant or animal that helps it blend in with its surroundings.

climate The weather of an area over a long period of time.

den An underground home for animals.

ecosystem All of the living and nonliving things in an area.

litter A group of young animals born to the same mother at one time.

pole One of two points on Earth that are farthest north or farthest south.

prey An animal that is hunted.

CONTENTS

1

LIFE IN THE ARCTIC

Not many animals on Earth can survive temperatures of –58 degrees Fahrenheit (–50 degrees Celsius). But the Arctic fox can! This amazing animal gets its name from the area where it lives: the **Arctic**. It is the area of Earth located near the North **Pole**.

Top of the World

The Arctic is marked on maps by an imaginary line called the Arctic Circle.

If you look at a globe, the Arctic is located at the top. Spin the globe and you'll see the entire area. Not many people live in this area because it gets so cold. Temperatures can get as low as –94°F (–70°C)!

The Arctic includes parts of Russia, Iceland, Sweden, Finland, Norway, Greenland, Canada, and the US state of Alaska.

A HARSH PLACE

The Arctic is a harsh **ecosystem.** Few animals can survive there. A large part of the Arctic is the frozen ocean waters of the Arctic Ocean. Walruses, seals, whales, and narwhals live under the frozen water. On land, polar bears, wolves, Arctic hare, reindeer, birds, and other animals share the ecosystem with the Arctic fox.

2

THE AMAZING ARCTIC FOX

The Arctic fox is known by different names around the world. It is sometimes called the white fox, snow fox, or polar fox. Fully grown, this furry little creature is no longer than 3 feet (1 meter) long from its nose to its fluffy tail.

AN ARCTIC TAIL

The Arctic fox's tail helps keep the animal safe in its surroundings. It also helps balance the animal when it jumps and pounces on **prey**. The tail also acts as a

The Arctic fox's long, bushy tail is also called a brush.

The Arctic fox's **camouflage** helps keep it from being seen easily by other animals.

warm cover during the cold winter weather. In fact, most of the fox's body parts and behaviors help it survive in the cold Arctic. Traits and behaviors that help an animal survive are called **adaptations**.

Getting Cozy

The Arctic fox has fur on the soles of its feet to keep it warm. A short face and ears also protect it from harsh cold weather.

CLEVER ADAPTATIONS

The Arctic fox has many adaptations to help it survive a cold **climate.** Climate is the typical weather over a period of time. The fur of the fox changes colors in different seasons. This is called camouflage. This helps the fox stay hidden from other animals. The fox's winter coat blends in with the snow. Its summer coat blends in with the ground and surroundings.

Some of the Arctic fox's adaptations include the way it behaves. It makes an

The Arctic fox
must act quickly
to catch a meal.

underground home called a **den.** This is a place where the fox can stay safe, especially during dangerous winter **blizzards**.

EATING IN THE ARCTIC

The Arctic fox is a good hunter. In the summer, its main diet is a small, mouse-sized animal called a lemming. The fox is fast. It can sprint up to 31 miles (50 kilometers) per hour. When it is ready to catch a meal, it jumps straight up in the air and pounces on its prey. The fox also has excellent hearing. It can hear small animals, such as the lemming, moving underneath the snow. The fox then dives face first into the snow to catch its prey. The Arctic fox also eats birds, bird eggs, hares, fish, and other small animals of the Arctic.

3

A YEAR WITH THE ARCTIC FOX

In the spring and summer, the Arctic fox is busy hunting for food. As the months pass, there are more and more hours of sunlight. The snow melts. Plants start to grow. Many animals move south to warmer temperatures where it is easier to find food. The fox's summer coat makes it harder for other animals to find it. Toward the end of the summer, the fox begins to save food for the winter months.

The color of the fox's fur changes during the four seasons in the Arctic.

SO MUCH SUNLIGHT

Because of Earth's tilt, the Arctic seasons are very unique. By the middle of June, the sun never really sets. It shines all day and night! Because of this, the Arctic is called the "land of the midnight sun."

A ROUGH WINTER

During the fall, the Arctic fox must prepare for the difficult winter ahead. It eats a lot so it can store body fat. During this time, the fox's body weight increases by half. This helps the animal stay warm in the cold. Once winter comes, the fox spends more time in its den to stay safe from blizzards. In the coldest months, the fox will follow larger animals such as the polar bear. It will eat the scraps of the food the polar bear leaves behind.

SO MUCH DARKNESS

The sun shines most of the time in Arctic summer. The opposite is true in the winter.

Highs and Lows

In the summer, temperatures change a lot throughout the Arctic. It can be 32°F (0°C) near the ocean. Areas inland can reach close to 70°F (21°C).

During winter, the Arctic fox has a harder time finding food.

There are many days when the sun is not seen at all. There is total darkness. This lack of sunlight is another reason the Arctic is one of the harshest places on Earth.

4

A FAMILY OF FOXES

Arctic foxes often hunt and travel on their own until they start a family. A young fox is called a kit. During the spring, foxes may build a new den where a **litter** can be born. There may be five to nine kits in a litter.

When the kits are born, they drink milk from their mother. They stay in the den for about a month. After they leave the den, they continue to drink milk from their mother for several more months. Both parents help raise the young foxes. When parents have more than one litter, older brothers and sisters also help raise the new kits.

Kits become adults in less than a year and live for three to six years.

Foxes come and go from their den using small entrances like this one.

Having the Blues

As an Arctic fox's coat changes colors, it can look blue. Because of this, the animal is sometimes called a blue fox. When Arctic foxes are born, they are either white or "blue."

A SAFE UNDERGROUND HOME

The underground dens Arctic foxes build last many years. Some dens are connected tunnels with many entrances. A large den can cover more than 10,760 square feet (1,000 square meters). That's larger than the infield of a baseball diamond! Some dens are so well made that they last for hundreds of years. They are used by many families of foxes. In every season, the Arctic fox shows why it is such an amazing creature.

ACTIVITY

MAKE AN ARCTIC FOOD WEB

Everything in an ecosystem is connected. A food web shows what animals in an ecosystem eat. When an animal eats another animal or plant, it gains energy. The energy flows through the ecosystem. A plant is eaten by a mouse. That mouse is then eaten by a rabbit. The energy from the plant moves to the mouse and then the rabbit.

You have just learned about the Arctic fox. Use what you learned to help you draw a food web like the one on the next page. Look at the names of a few of the animals that live in